Even Inks Need Friends

by Michael Scotto
illustrated by The Ink Circle

Welcome to Midlandia
Our Story Begins

Midlandia University

Community Center

Animal Land

HERE

Town Square

Playland Park

Bike Factory

Harvest Farms

STARRING

WILDA
WANNADOGOOD
THE ZOOKEEPER

A VERY
SPECIAL INK

Midlandia looked like the perfect town, and in many ways, it was. Its hills were beautiful. Its citizens, the Midlandians, were hard-working and happy. But Midlandia did have a problem. Deep under ground, under the surface...

...lived the Inks! The Inks were not hard-working.
They spent all of their time playing.

But for the Inks, "playing" meant playing tricks on the Midlandians. **"Help!"** cried Buck the banker. "Those Inks have caught my foot in a rope!"

"**Oh, yuck!**" cried Brick the builder. "Those Inks have filled my hardhat with mud."

Every week, the Inks would gather
and plan new pranks to play.
  "Let's go to the art gallery," said one,
"and make Ink prints on the paintings."
  "Let's sneak into the library," said
another, "and turn the books all topsy-turvy!"
  But the eldest Ink was not impressed.
"These are tricks we've played before," he
answered with a snort.

Then, something odd happened. An Ink who had never spoken before, a quiet, shy, little Ink, decided to pipe up. "I have an idea," he said. "One that would shock the socks off those Midlandians!"

The others' ears perked up on end. They all leaned in to listen. "What if..." began the shy Ink. "What if we creep into town in the darkest of night, and do something...nice?"

The Inks all burst into laughter! "Do something nice?" asked the eldest Ink. "Who ever heard of such nonsense?"

"**I mean it!**" said the shy Ink. "We could leave presents in every house in town. Or better yet, we could invite the Midlandians down here for Inksgiving dinner!"

The eldest Ink became very upset. **"Stop that, you!"** he shouted. "I will not have such talk in my cave. We are Inks, and Inks are not nice! If you can't say something mean, then don't say anything at all."

"Who says we always have to be mean?" asked the shy Ink.

The eldest Ink did not have a good answer, so he grew steaming mad. **"Out! Get out!"** he roared. "You are banished from this place."

"Banished?" asked the shy Ink.

"Banished!" the eldest Ink repeated. "That means you are no longer welcome here. Get your things, and go now."

The shy Ink wandered sadly through the cold,
rainy town square. He already missed his Ink friends,
and he had nowhere to stay.

Soon, the Ink saw a sign he could read. "Animal
Land," he read with a shiver. "I am like an animal...
maybe I can stay here." And into Animal Land he crept.

Early the next morning, Wilda the zookeeper came to work. "There is so much to do!" she thought. "Animals to feed, plants to care for, tours to give! I'll start by feeding the lizards."

Wilda opened the pantry door and saw every animal's food right where it belonged. But she also saw something that didn't belong.

"An Ink!"
Wilda screamed. The Ink arched his back, as if ready to attack.

To Wilda's surprise, the Ink just let out a sneeze. "Excuse me!" he said. "I'm sorry to intrude like this, but...ach-oo!" The Ink sniffled. "May I please explain?"

Wilda gave the Ink some hot soup and a tissue for his stuffy nose. "This is an Ink of a different color," she thought as he finished telling his story.

"I miss my friends, but I can't go back home," said the Ink. **"Will you be my friend?"**

Wilda felt sorry for the poor little fellow, but she was still not sure if she could trust him. He was, after all, an Ink. "I don't know if Midlandians and Inks can be friends," she said. "Well, then," said the Ink, **"do you need a helper?"**

Wilda decided to give the Ink a chance. "You can be my assistant for the day," she said. "Let's begin by feeding these iguanas."

"I'm not going near those things!" shrieked the Ink. "**They'll swallow me whole!**"

"**Don't worry**, little Ink," Wilda explained. "Iguanas might look scary, but they only like vegetables."

The Ink helped Wilda
feed every lizard, bird, and
fish in record time.
"What a wonderful
helper!" she thought. "But
where has he gone now?"

The Ink reappeared, holding a beautiful bunch of flowers. "I picked you the prettiest ones I could find!" he said.

But Wilda pinched her nose. "They're quite lovely," she said, "but boy, are they stinky!"

"I can't smell a thing," replied the Ink.

"That's because you have a cold, silly!" said Wilda. "It was a nice thought...but pee-eww!"

Soon, the zoo was ready to open for visitors.
"Thanks for your help," said Wilda.

"I'd be happy to stay as your assistant," offered the Ink.

"I have a better idea," Wilda replied. "Why don't you stay as my friend?"

"Really?" asked the Ink with a smile.

"My only problem now is...how will I explain this to everyone else?" wondered Wilda.

"That could be hard," agreed the Ink. "But you could try telling them this."

"Not everything can be known at first look.
You can't read one page and know the whole book.
Cute things can be mean, and scary things nice.
That's why it's good to always look twice.
What I knew at the start has changed by the end,
And that's why this Ink is now my new friend."

DISCUSSION QUESTIONS

Have you made any new friends this year? How did you meet?

What was the last thing that made you feel surprised?
Why did it surprise you?

EVEN INKS NEED FRIENDS

Revised edition. First printing, January 2010.
© 2016 Lincoln Learning Solutions
294 Massachusetts Avenue
Rochester, PA 15074
Visit us on the web at http://www.lincolnlearningsolutions.org.
Midlandia® is a registered trademark of Lincoln Learning Solutions.

Edited by Ashley Mortimer
Character design by Evette Gabriel
Environmental design by Joshua Perry

EVEN INKS NEED FRIENDS

by Michael Scotto

illustrated by The Ink Circle